IMAGES
of America

ALAMEDA COUNTY
SHERIFF'S OFFICE

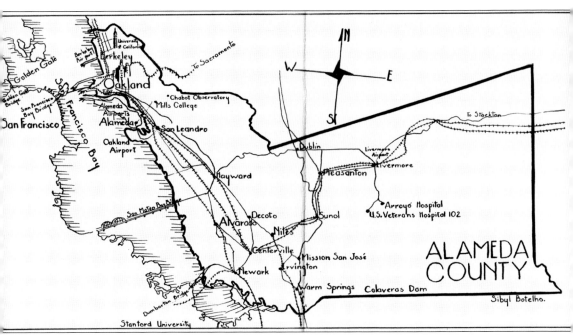

Alameda County is seen here as it appeared around 1937. When the county was formed in 1853, it had about 8,000 residents, with most of them living in the Oakland and San Leandro areas. It was primarily an agricultural economy. The most prevalent crimes were cattle rustling and theft, but murders and assaults were not uncommon along the few roads going east to the Central Valley. The sheriff was usually the only law enforcement officer, and he had only a few deputies to cover the entire county. By the end of the 20th century, the sheriff's office faced a dramatically more complicated situation. Alameda County had over 1.4 million residents and a very diversified economy. Traveling around and through the county was much easier. It was well connected to San Francisco, the rest of the Bay Area, and the rest of the county by bridges, ferries, railroads, freeways, and airports. The sheriff's office had evolved from six-shooters and horses to semi-automatic pistols, patrol cars, radios, and computers. (Author's collection.)

ON THE COVER: Staff of the Alameda County Sheriff's Department are pictured in front of the county jail at 491 Washington Street between Fourth and Fifth Streets in Oakland, California, in November 1936. At center in the first row is Sheriff Michael B. Driver, who served from 1930 through 1940. In 1936, his salary was $600 per month. His secretary, Vera Morton (first row, far right), made $140 per month while deputies made $190 per month. (Courtesy of the Alameda County Sheriff's Archive, Alameda County Sheriff's Office, California.)

IMAGES
of America

ALAMEDA COUNTY
SHERIFF'S OFFICE

Steven S. Minniear

ARCADIA
PUBLISHING

Published by Arcadia Publishing
Charleston, South Carolina

Printed in the United States of America

Library of Congress Control Number: 2023944369

For all general information, please contact Arcadia Publishing:
Telephone 843-853-2070
Fax 843-853-0044
E-mail sales@arcadiapublishing.com

Visit us on the Internet at www.arcadiapublishing.com

This book is dedicated to the staff, present and past, of the Alameda County Sheriff's Office, whose commitment to serving and protecting the communities of Alameda County is inspiring and appreciated. To those who gave their all, we cannot thank you enough.

CONTENTS

ACKNOWLEDGMENTS

I would like to thank many people and institutions for making this book possible. If it is true that it takes a village to raise a child, then it is also true that it takes a community to write a book. I've been fortunate to be part of a very generous community of retired deputy sheriffs and staff who are proud of where they worked. They took that pride one step further and worked to collect, preserve, and present the history of the Alameda County Sheriff's Office in the sheriff's archive. Special thanks go to Dale Toussaint, Ralph Streicher, Pat Adams, Greg Rees, Jim Knudsen, J.D. Nelson, Ray Kelly, Mary Matzek, Bill Rhodes, and Bud Harlan, who graciously shared their stories and passion with me, the historian guy. Also, thanks to former sheriff Gregory Ahern and current sheriff Yesenia Sanchez for their support of the sheriff's archive. Finally, thanks to my wife for all her support as she listened far too often to the question, "Guess what I saw at the archives today." Most of the photographs in this book come from the Alameda County Sheriff's Archive. Other photographs have their origins mentioned at the end of the caption. Thanks to all those institutions that allowed me to share their images with the public.

INTRODUCTION

Located on the eastern shore of San Francisco Bay, Alameda County is now the home or the workplace for well over a million people. During its history, Native Americans, Spanish explorers, Mexican ranchers, miners on their way to (or home from) the California Gold Rush, rancheros, farmers, business owners, railroad tycoons, land speculators, and others lived, worked, and played within its borders. And with all those people came the need for law and order.

California became a state in 1850, but Alameda County was not one of the original counties. After heavy lobbying by politically connected local groups around San Jose and Oakland, it was carved out of the northern portion of Santa Clara and the southern portion of Contra Costa Counties. The county's first election for officers took place in May 1853. Any eligible voter (at that time, only men) was able to run for office. As author M.W. Wood noted in his 1883 history of the county, "This election was long known as the "steeple chase" for there were from five to six candidates for each office, while many of the would-be county officers appeared in the poll-lists under nicknames." One of those candidates became the first sheriff, Andrew H. Broder.

Broder faced a daunting task. With only himself and a few deputies, he was responsible for maintaining law and order over 821 square miles. His jurisdiction extended from San Francisco Bay over two ranges of hills to the beginning of the great California Central Valley. With only 3,000 inhabitants in 1853, the county was so sparsely populated that the number of cattle far exceeded that of people. Besides that, the county had a history of lawlessness. Cattle rustling was widespread, and stagecoaches and freight traffic were easy targets for robbery. And the geography was very rugged, making travel slow and difficult. For those wishing to evade capture, the inland hills had many difficult-to-search valleys.

Since 1853, the 23 sheriffs and the organization have adapted to the times as the county changed. And the county and the nearby Bay Area changed dramatically. Just some of the challenges facing sheriffs in these times were the end of the Gold Rush, the Civil War, the arrival of the transcontinental railroad, periodic economic depressions and recessions, labor strikes, the Spanish-American War, World War I, Prohibition, the Great Depression, World War II, the Cold War, Vietnam, public protests and riots, and periodic increases (and decreases) in crime. The sheriff and staff have responded to innumerable accidents, structure fires and wildfires, and earthquakes, not the least of which were the 1868, 1906, and 1989 earthquakes.

According to the county charter, the sheriff is the chief law enforcement officer of the county. The sheriff's powers include all the duties prescribed by state law including the responsibility to sponsor, supervise, or practice crime prevention, rehabilitation of persons previously convicted of a crime, and the suppression of delinquency; arrest and take before a magistrate all persons who attempt to commit or have committed a public offense; prevent and suppress affrays, breaches of the peace, riots, and insurrections; command the aid of as many inhabitants as necessary in the execution of his/her duties; have charge of and keep the county jail and the prisoners in it; supply ambulance service; have custody and disposition of prisoners' property and valuables; perform other acts necessary to preserve the peace of the county; and search for and rescue persons who are lost or are in danger of their lives within or in the immediate vicinity of the county. The sheriff is also the coroner of Alameda County, the director of emergency services, and an officer of the courts.

Formed with the appointment of its first sheriff, the Alameda County Sheriff's Office grew from a single sheriff riding horses through mainly agricultural land to a modern law enforcement agency serving a highly populated residential, commercial, and industrial landscape. Today, the sheriff's office serves over one and a half million residents using the latest technology and practices. The office has more than 1,500 authorized positions, which include over 1,000 sworn personnel.

This book is not a complete history of the Alameda County Sheriff's Office. It is a journey through the years looking at the photographic record of some aspects of the office. The chapters are organized to tell some of the stories and provide descriptions of the many people, places, events, and equipment related to the office's evolution. It includes images of the sheriffs and some of the hundreds of deputies, recruits, staff, families, prisoners, and the public who were part of the office's story. It also includes places important to the sheriff's operations, such as courthouses, jails, and stations. The book also highlights some of the major and minor events of the county's law enforcement story. Finally, there are images showing the uniforms, transportation, and gear used by the office over the years.

Most of the interesting photographs shown here were collected and preserved at the office's archive and illustrate the history of hundreds of deputies dealing with a multitude of events ranging from the horrific to the mundane, and sometimes the humorous. This book will explore the changing face of law enforcement as the office and its staff dealt with crime, earthquakes, anti–Vietnam War demonstrations, sports events, parades, traffic, accidents, and all the other adventures that make up a deputy's typical day. And readers will find out how the riot squad's name came to be the same as the villains in a 1968 motion picture.

The complete history of the office has yet to be written. Until that is done, I hope you like this small portion of that history that has been selected for your viewing.

Throughout this book, you will see three different terms used for the sheriff and his or her staff: sheriff, sheriff's department, and sheriff's office. At first, the sheriff's organization was just the sheriff and a few deputies. They were commonly and collectively referred to as "the sheriff." Later, as the staff became larger and more professional, the organization became known as the sheriff's department. During the tenure of sheriff/coroner Charles Plummer, the name was formally changed to the sheriff's office. Sheriff Plummer was said to believe that being a directly elected official of the county, his organization was most appropriately titled an office.

One

PEOPLE

SHERIFFS, DEPUTIES, RECRUITS, STAFF, FAMILIES, PRISONERS, AND PUBLIC

The tale of the Alameda County Sheriff's Office is really an accumulation of the stories of the sheriffs, deputies, and staff who served in it. Some of those stories were captured in photographs. This chapter tells just a few of the recorded stories that shaped the sheriff's office and Alameda County.

The early sheriffs and deputies only had a passing influence on its history. Every two to four years, through one or many two-year election cycles, sheriffs came to office, hired a few deputies (usually family or friends), enrolled or certified special deputies, and enforced the laws. From 1853 through the end of the 1900s, the sheriff had few full-time staff, and the sheriff himself often did the work.

Alameda County's location across the bay from San Francisco meant it was used by many people and much freight. It was the main land route to the Central Valley and the Sierra Nevada mountains. Gold, grain, cattle, and their owners traveled through these vast, empty spaces. Cattle and sheep rustlers were a constant problem. Criminals found shelter in the rugged and sparsely populated hill country. The few small towns offered gambling, liquor, and a place to sell stolen goods. Some of the early sheriffs, especially Harry Morse, parlayed their exploits tracking and capturing desperadoes into fame, if not fortune. The bad guys also developed well-known reputations, in part due to the San Francisco and Sacramento papers and others publishing sensational stories. Joaquin Murietta and Tiburcio Vasquez were two of the more notorious outlaws whose exploits or deaths captured headlines.

Later, as the county became more populated and roads and railroads increased the ease of travel, a new kind of sheriff developed. Staff grew, and eventually, professionalism replaced the more informal nature of policing. Training, techniques, and technology improved the deputy sheriff's ability to protect the community. Along the way, there were interesting people and stories that told the history of the sheriff's department and the communities they served.

Alameda County was established in March 1853 out of parts of northern Santa Clara County and southern Contra Costa County. In May 1853, Andrew Henderson Broder won the first election for county sheriff. Less than a year later, he appeared in this photograph with his new bride, Sarah Ann Smith. (Washington Township Museum of Local History.)

H.N. "Harry" Morse was Alameda County's fourth sheriff. He is arguably the most famous early sheriff. This is in part due to his efforts to self-promote his exploits, as well as subsequent biographies. He served from 1863 to 1877. He famously ended the careers of various criminals including Narato Ponce and Juan Soto.

ANDREW BRODER
1853-57

WHATTAN E. EDMUNDSO
1857-61

J.A. MAYHEW
1861-63

H.N. MORSE
1863-77

JEREMIAH TYRREL
1877-82

CHARLES McCLEVERTY
1882-84

W.E. HALE
1884-90

W.H.H. HUSSEY
1890-92

ROBERT McKILLICAN
1892-94

C.B. WHITE
1894-98

Here are the first through tenth Alameda County sheriffs. From the creation of the county in 1853 through the end of the 19th century, these men oversaw a steadily growing county population and changing economy. By the 1890s, the county was still primarily rural and agricultural, but there were fewer and fewer cattle. Cattle rustling remained a serious crime, but murder, assault, and theft increasingly became issues outside the towns. Some of the sheriffs were more memorable than others. Andrew Broder was the first, and led the investigation into the first major robbery in the county, when someone robbed the Alameda County treasury of over $11,000, all the money the county had in 1855. Sheriff Harry Morse chased murderers and thieves throughout the state. His exploits resulted in books being written about him. The publicity later allowed him to become the most well-known detective in California. During C.B. White's tenure, several deputies were killed when a gunpowder plant blew up. The person who blew up the plant and a bystander were also killed.

OSCAR ROGERS
1898-1902

JOHN N. BISHOP
1902-06

FRANK BARNET
1906-26

BURTON F. BECKER
1926-30

GRANT D. MILLER
6 days 1930
expired term of BEC

M. B. DRIVER
1930-40

H. P. "Jack" Gleason
1940-1963

Frank I. Madigan
1963-1975

1975-1979
T. L. HOUCHINS, SHERIFF

Glen Dyer
1979-1987

The 11th through 20th sheriffs operated through most of the 20th century. They faced the increasing urbanization of the county, tremendous population growth, and a corresponding increase in crime. Alameda County became an even more important hub for the Bay Area economy with the completion of a bridge from San Francisco to Oakland. Two world wars, several smaller wars, Prohibition, the Great Depression, recessions, two major earthquakes, two horrific fires, and tumultuous demonstrations and riots made their tenures challenging.

The 21st through 23rd sheriffs had to deal with many developments at the end of the 20th century and the beginning of the 21st century. For Sheriff Charles Plummer (left), local, national, and international issues resulted in demonstrations by thousands of people. Only a few of those demonstrations included violence. At the same time, dramatic increases in the population often led to increases in crime and incarceration. He and the office also opened the new Santa Rita Jail, which had its own set of challenges. That was soon followed by the dramatic effects of the 1989 Loma Prieta earthquake. Then the terrorist attacks of September 11, 2001, gave rise to a whole new range of concerns that resulted in changing the types of equipment used by the sheriff's office and requiring new levels of mutual aid. For Sheriff Gregory Ahern (center), increasing urbanization and suburbanization led to continued dramatic increases in population, sometimes with a corresponding increase in crime. And in 2022, the voters of Alameda County elected their first female sheriff, Yesenia Sanchez. Many of the same issues faced by her predecessors will likely make her tenure just as challenging.

VOTE FOR

Frank Barnet

(Incumbent)

CANDIDATE FOR

SHERIFF

Primary Election August 29, 1922

9

Frank Barnet was the 13th sheriff and was elected in 1906. He served until 1926, losing a closely fought race to Burton Becker, the Piedmont chief of police. Becker's supporters had tried to connect Barnet to the murder of a young woman, claiming she was his mistress. Later, newspaper reports stated the young woman had been "dating" different well-to-do men and received money from each of them. The murder was never solved.

A senior leader of the local Ku Klux Klan, Burton Becker became sheriff in 1926 on a "clean government" platform after running a vicious campaign against Frank Barnet. His tenure was scandal-ridden, as he ran a protection racket for illegal liquor distributors and gambling interests. In 1930, Alameda County district attorney Earl Warren accused him of multiple criminal violations. He was convicted and served time in San Quentin State Prison.

H.P. "Jack" Gleason was the longest-serving sheriff in Alameda County history. Elected in 1940, he retired in 1963. As the 17th sheriff, he served through dramatic changes in the county that had huge impacts on law enforcement. He may have been one of the most consequential sheriffs due to his attempts to incorporate rehabilitation into incarceration. He also established the Santa Rita Rehabilitation Center near Dublin, California.

Sheriff Gleason rides with a posse in this undated photograph. In another photograph at a different time, a newspaper correspondent accurately noted, "Sheriff H.P. Gleason colorfully customed [sic] in western regalia, leads the Alameda County Sheriffs [sic] Posse." The sheriff appeared like this in public events throughout the county during his tenure.

Sheriff Frank I. Madigan (far left) leads former sheriff Gleason through the inspection of the staff. This was a special event marking Gleason's retirement in 1963. The image captures a moment in the history of the department as the last civilian sheriff was replaced by a sheriff who had been in law enforcement throughout his working life. It reflects the increasing professionalization of the department, an effort fostered by Sheriff Gleason.

Madigan succeeded Gleason as the 18th sheriff in January 1963. He continued many traditions, including being a prominent participant in the sheriff's posse. Like Gleason, Madigan used the posse as a community goodwill gesture, often riding at the head of the posse in local parades. His tenure ended in 1975 and included one of the most turbulent periods in the department's history.

Sometimes no job is too small for the sheriff, especially when it is near election time or positive publicity is needed. In 1967, Sheriff Madigan poses on a ladder with a $50 reward sign at the entrance of Old St. Raymond's church in Dublin. The historic church and the nearby cemetery were the scenes of vandalism and residents wanted help in ending the damage.

A young boy watches Constable Manuel Borge of Eden Township pose with his two bloodhounds. Trixie and Pet were available to track down suspects in 1913. They were his personal pets and not official members of local law enforcement. As an elected township constable, Borge was a law enforcement officer who came under dual direction from the sheriff and the local justice of the peace.

The sheriff's department was not the only law enforcement agency working in the far corners of Alameda County. Each township had one or more locally elected constables. Henry R. Seeband was the Murray Township constable in 1922. One newspaper account reported how the constable and his trusty vehicle followed a train from Livermore to Niles to take a robber into custody. (Livermore Heritage Guild.)

FORMER CONSTABLE OF EDEN TOWNSHIP

Primary Election, August 31, 1926
General Election, Nov. 2, 1926

VOTE FOR

M. BORGE

FOR

CONSTABLE

EDEN TOWNSHIP

Your Assistance will be Appreciated

Manuel Borge's career highlights how different law enforcement was in the early 1900s. Rather than being appointed by the sheriff, constables were officers elected in townships but were concurrently considered deputy sheriffs. After serving as a deputy constable for several years, Borge was elected constable for Eden Township in 1911. He lost the position in the 1914 election, then ran for office again in 1926 but lost.

In November 1936, the staff of the Alameda County Sheriff's Department poses for a group photograph outside what was then already called the "Old County Jail," between Fourth and Fifth Streets in Oakland. To the left of Sheriff Michael B. Driver (first row, center) sits Undersheriff Hugo Radbruch. Included among the 48 staff was a future sheriff, Frank Madigan (second row, second from left).

Posing proudly behind the sheriff's department communications van with high-tech Motorola portable telephones are five of the staff members who helped keep the department linked together. From left to right are Sgt. Bill Wehe, Capt. Claude Marchand, Art Allen (sitting in van), Sgt. Gene Davidson (California Highway Patrol), Capt. C. Brower McMurphy, and Lt. George Wisner.

Standing at attention for an inspection are participants in the Regular Basic Course, 83rd Academy, at the Alameda County Sheriff's Academy in Dublin, which took place between October and September 1984. Training is a critical component of law enforcement. Even in the 1960s and 1970s, academy training was extensive, with over 200 hours of instruction. The intensive experience forged friendships and collaborative relationships for the rest of many deputies' careers.

Minna F. Ralph started duty as the department's first woman hired as a deputy sheriff on September 20, 1944. Newspaper articles describing her career include stories of undercover work, various postings in the department, and service at the Santa Rita Jail. By 1950, Ralph was a lieutenant in charge of women's detention activities.

September 20, 1944
DATED

May 14, 1910
DATE OF BIRTH

5' 8½"   180
HEIGHT   WEIGHT

Blue   Blonde
COLOR-EYES   COLOR-HAIR

Fair
COMPLEXION

OTHER OBVIOUS PHYSICAL CHARACTERISTICS THAT WILL AID IN IDENTIFICATION

In the 1950s, Minna Ralph continued to progress through the ranks and became a captain. She is pictured here with her staff (from left to right) Lynette Warren, Mary Olsen, Edna Weiss, Captain Ralph, Omega Rogers, and B. Devereaux. According to a 1959 *Oakland Tribune* article, Ralph had 16 deputies working for her.

Sheriff Gleason (far left) and Captain Ralph review the deputies under Ralph's command at Santa Rita Jail near Dublin on July 29, 1959. Ralph and her unit operated the women's section at the jail. They were responsible for all female inmates. By 1960, there were 16 women deputies, and the department was recruiting more.

For years, women were not authorized to be deputy sheriffs. Nevertheless, there was a need for women to monitor female inmates at the jail. They were known as matrons. By the time of this photograph in 1970, (from left to right) Roberta Mueller, Phyllis Christ, Thelma Brake, and Beverly Cervone were fully authorized deputies and posed in their uniforms at the Rowell Ranch Rodeo.

In a staged photo, Deputy Sheriff Sharon Penn cites Sheriff Tom Houchins while Deputy Roberta Mello observes from the curb. The photograph was taken to commemorate the beginning of female deputies performing patrol activities. Women had been deputies since 1944, but they were not patrol officers until 1975.

Lanier Temple was the first African American hired by the sheriff's office, in 1931. He served in many positions during his career. Promoted to lieutenant in 1950, he became the commanding officer at the Santa Rita Jail in 1954. He was promoted to captain in July 1956 and later became chief jailer. Captain Temple retired on January 1, 1959, after 27 years of service.

Until the late 1940s, each local Bay Area police and sheriff department trained its officers using its own standards and practices. The quality of the training varied widely. Sheriff Gleason and his staff felt that by pooling resources, local law enforcement agencies could improve officer training, which would also improve the quality of law enforcement services to the communities they served. Realizing that having each local agency do their own training was also costly and inefficient, Sheriff Gleason worked to create the Northern California Peace Officers Training Center on the grounds of Santa Rita Jail. In early 1947, the first class poses outside the main training building.

Instructors and students participate in an accident investigation exercise near the Alameda County storehouses on the grounds of Santa Rita Jail. Located along the busy and accident-prone two-lane US Highway 50, there were plenty of damaged cars to use for staged accidents. This exercise may have been part of the first regional training class offered in early 1947.

A badly beat-up storefront dummy acts as a mock body during crime scene training. In 1947, the regional training center used whatever props they could find to stage a scene. In a far cry from modern law enforcement techniques and technology, papers, pens, and clipboards are used to describe and document the situation.

Here are more examples of the differences between the first regional law enforcement basic course and modern standards. Then, attendees wore whatever they wanted, including a Hawaiian shirt. One is outfitted in his local uniform, complete with a hat. Today, uniforms are purchased by recruits. Another difference is the blackboard and chalk, and notes taken with pen and paper.

This c. 1950 image shows a class preparing for baton instruction. Four trainees wear the leather jackets and khaki trousers they probably wore during their prior military service.

26

Among the most interesting volunteer units within the sheriff's department was the air squadron, sometimes referred to as the aero squadron. It included deputies and volunteers who had pilot's licenses and airplanes. The squadron was used for search and rescue as well as civil defense duties and transporting prisoners. Deputy Jim Young sometimes flew prisoners to various jails throughout California. In the 1950s and 1960s, he would land and take off from one of the abandoned streets near Santa Rita Jail.

The first Alameda County Sheriff's Department Academy class poses for their graduation photograph on the steps of the Santa Rita Administration Building. The class was held in January 1958 on the grounds near the original Santa Rita Jail. It replaced the earlier regional training academy and used many of the same locations.

Deputies of the aero squadron pose in front of one of the aircraft used to support the sheriff's department in the early 1950s. After World War II, many veterans returned to civilian life with either pilot training or a desire to become a pilot. One way to use those flying skills was as a volunteer with the sheriff's department. The aircraft were all privately owned, operated, and maintained, and the squadron worked out of local airports. In the 1950s and early 1960s, Alameda County had a

much smaller population and there were small airports scattered around the county. In addition, there were many privately owned landing fields. Seen here from left to right are (kneeling) John Maggi, unidentified, Howard Garner, and Bud Rankin; (standing) Gedree Faulkner, John Sakajian, unidentified, Lt. Jerry Hagan, Walter Stamett, Bob Giordanio, Herb Jacobs, unidentified, and Wally Fields.

Another staged training shot shows one of every law enforcement officer's worst fears: a traffic stop gone bad. The background indicates the photograph was taken near Santa Rita Jail. The Quonset hut was one of the buildings left over from World War II when the jail property was part of the US Naval Training and Distribution Center, Shoemaker (also known as Camp Shoemaker).

Here is the appropriate resolution of the training exercise above. The suspect is handcuffed and put in the back of the waiting vehicle. His ride to the jail will be short, since it can be seen in the background. A guard in the jail tower, just visible at right, may have watched the entire scene.

A civil defense team, including volunteers and sheriff's office staff, conducts an exercise during the 1960s. A vast amount of surplus US military equipment became available for cities, counties, and states after World War II. Alameda County had a large amount of surplus government property available to use for exercises, including buildings near the Santa Rita Jail.

Deputies practice on the firing range at Camp Parks. Before upgraded ranges were built near Santa Rita Jail, the department used the pistol and shotgun ranges at Camp Parks. Training and qualification standards for firearms were the same for women and men. The date of this photograph is unknown, but it could be from the late 1950s or 1960s.

Training, especially with firearms, is a critical part of law enforcement. Equipment, training, and practices change, sometimes dramatically, over time. This photograph shows a late 1950s training exercise with Deputy Bud Garrigan (left) and Lt. Carl Dean at the range with a revolver and the then-appropriate method for shooting. The sheriff's office issued Smith & Wesson Model 66 revolvers for many years.

This is another view of the same training session in the late 1950s at the ranges near either Santa Rita Jail or Camp Parks. Firearm ranges for many years were primitive. The current ranges just behind Santa Rita Jail are far more advanced and are used by several law enforcement agencies when not in use by the sheriff's office.

The training given to deputies has changed over the years as equipment and situations they face have changed. Simple drills at the range are still necessary but are supplemented by more advanced training for high-risk situations such as hostage recovery. Here, deputies practice tactics for clearing a building using a distraction device (commonly known as flash bangs).

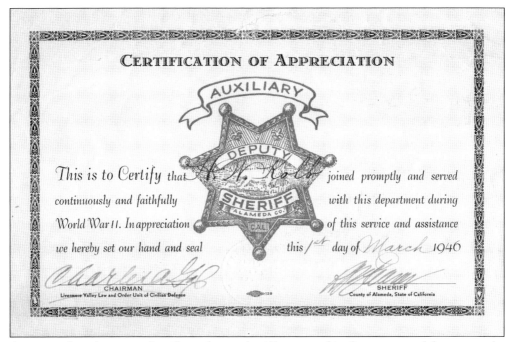

At a time when there were few, if any, deputy sheriffs on patrol in distant parts of the county, the office depended on volunteer and unpaid auxiliaries to assist in limited law enforcement duties. Local Dublin farmer Harold Kolb served as one of these volunteers for many years. Here is a certification of appreciation from Sheriff Gleason for Kolb's service. (Dublin Heritage Park & Museums.)

Alameda County reserve deputy sheriffs reload weapons during firearms training. The reserve deputies met the same firearms qualifications as full-time deputies. Firearms training and qualification were done on their own time, often on weekends. In June 1973, training was held at the firearms range at Camp Parks, Dublin.

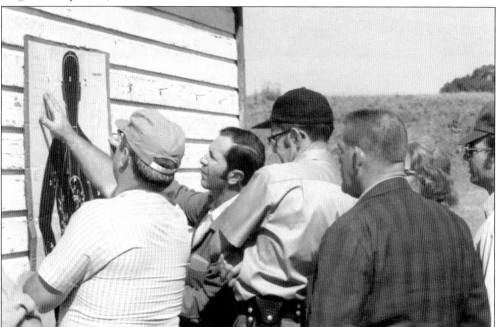

Reserve deputy sheriffs and instructors check firearms qualification scores in 1973. The qualification courses often had an instruction component included on the day of shooting. Reserve deputies were just as concerned as full-time deputies about shooting the highest scores possible. The competition between reserve deputies during the day's qualification could be quite intense.

Graduates of the Regular Basic Course, 42nd Academy, pose for a class photo at Santa Rita, California, on March 26, 1974. The different uniforms reflect the various local and state law enforcement agencies that took advantage of the training offered by the sheriff's office. Note the uniforms worn by female deputies in the 1970s.

A deputy's job is more than just patrol or jail duty. Reaching out to the community to suggest ways to avoid crime is part of their work. Participating in community events at fairs, farmers' markets, parades, and similar occasions often involves deputies and volunteers. At this event, crime prevention information was supplemented with a poster asking for the public's help in locating a young Dublin girl, Ilene Misheloff, kidnapped in 1989. The case remains unsolved.

The original Santa Rita Jail was on the grounds of a former US Navy base. After the Navy left, Alameda County took possession of the land. The property included former officer's quarters, which were small houses with garages. The sheriff's department staff working at the jail had the opportunity to live in these buildings. Pictured is Lt. Louis Seiferth's home in 1959. In the background on the left are the barracks at Parks Air Force Base. In a coincidence, Seiferth separated from the Navy in 1946 near this same location.

One of the advantages of working at Santa Rita Jail was that family housing was provided nearby. Here, three-month-old Ramona poses with her mother in 1947 on the porch of what had been, just a short while ago, a Navy officer's home. Anchors still decorate the window shutters.

A Santa Rita Jail deputy's children play outside his house in April 1948. The house appears to be close to the boundary with the former Camp Parks or Camp Shoemaker. The Quonset huts left over from the Navy may be storage used by the county or by the jail. Mount Diablo looms in the distance.

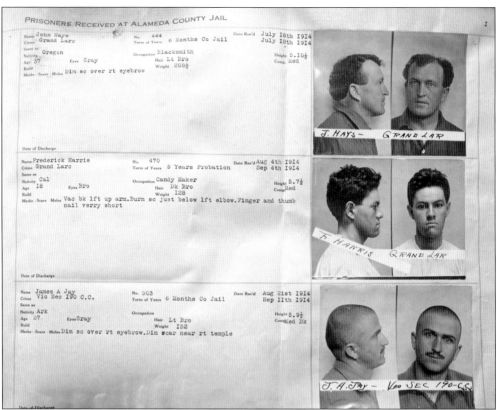

Name John Hays
Crime Grand Larc
Same as
Nativity Oregon
Age 37   Eyes Gray
Build
Marks—Scars—Moles Dim sc over rt eyebrow
No. 444   Term of Years 6 Months Co Jail
Occupation Blacksmith
Hair Lt Bro
Weight 209½
Date Rec'd July 18th 1914
July 18th 1914
Height 5.10½
Comp. Med

J. HAYS — GRAND LAR

Date of Discharge

Name Frederick Harris
Crime Grand Larc
Same as
Nativity Cal
Age 18   Eyes Bro
Build
Marks—Scars—Moles Vac bk lft up arm.Burn sc just below lft elbow.Finger and thumb nail verry short
No. 470   Term of Years 5 Years Probation
Occupation Candy Maker
Hair Dk Bro
Weight 128
Date Rec'd Aug 4th 1914
Sep 4th 1914
Height 5.7½
Comp. Med

F. HARRIS   GRAND LAR

Date of Discharge

Name James A Jay
Crime Vio Sec 190 C.C.
Same as
Nativity Ark
Age 27   Eyes Gray
Build
Marks—Scars—Moles Dim sc over rt eyebrow.Dim scar near rt temple
No. 503   Term of Years 6 Months Co Jail
Occupation
Hair Lt Bro
Weight 152
Date Rec'd Aug 21st 1914
Sep 11th 1914
Height 5.9½
Comp. Med Dk

J.H.Jay — Vao Sec 190-C.C.

Date of Discharge

The processing of arrestees and the documentation of their history in the law enforcement system has developed over the years. Mugshots and other photographs were an early development in that process. This page identifies three prisoners received at the Alameda County Jail in July and August 1914. The information on John Hays, Frederick Harris, and James Jay includes their physical descriptions, occupations, crimes, and sentences.

This is a 20th-century postcard purporting to show an actual photograph of the famous California bandit Joaquin Murietta. Alleged to be a robber and murderer, he was later portrayed as a Hispanic Robin Hood. Murietta was often the focus of popular attention. He frequented the area of eastern Alameda County in the early 1850s, and died in a shootout with another California law enforcement officer, Harry Love, in 1853.

December 1908 was not a good month for W.T. Williams, A.L. Orr, and Bud Rivers, who found themselves in San Quentin as prisoners 23206, 23207, and 23208, respectively. They received sentences ranging from one to two years for embezzlement and forgery. For many years, San Quentin housed most longer-term prisoners from Alameda County. The official record of prisoners can be found in this early 20th century volume now stored at the sheriff's archive. These detailed notes describe prisoners' physical appearance in order to positively identify them. Notes include height, age, eye color, hair color, complexion, weight, foot size, and hat size. The relatively recent introduction of photography allowed San Quentin to match text with photographs.

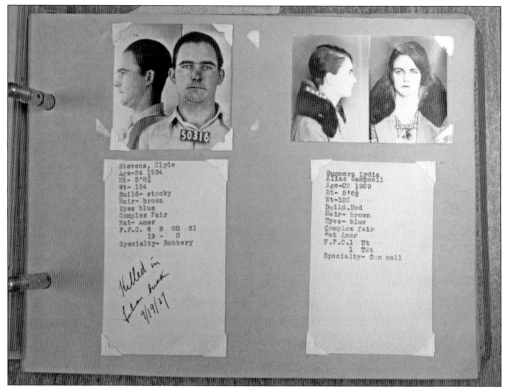

For many years, the sheriff's office had an identification and modus operandi file to keep track of people deputies were likely to come across, including Clyde Stevens and Lydia Summers. This mugshot book identifies Stevens and his specialty, robbery. Summers, alias Lydia Sampsell, is identified with her specialty, being a gun moll.

Sheriff Gleason swears in Fleet Admiral Chester W. Nimitz as a special deputy around 1947. Admiral Nimitz commanded US Navy forces in much of the Pacific during World War II. Gleason was always interested in photo opportunities with influential, famous people. At this time, Nimitz was chief of naval operations and the commanding Navy officer for the entire country. What he thought about becoming an honorary deputy sheriff was not recorded.

To
My very good
friend —
Sheriff
Gleason —
My best
Jack

Sheriff Gleason was an expert in public relations. A tireless advocate for the sheriff's department and Alameda County, Gleason took time to participate in several law enforcement associations and civic groups. He cultivated many friends and associates, especially celebrities. Ever aware of current events, he met and became friends with television actor, director, and producer Jack Webb, famous for his police-themed shows *Dragnet* and *Adam-12*. In the sheriff's archive, there are images of Gleason with other celebrities, including Casey Stengel, Billy Martin, and Earl Warren.

While working as a Dublin police officer, Deputy John Paul Monego was shot and killed while responding to a robbery and hostage situation in Dublin on December 19, 1998. He was not the last deputy to die while on duty.

As of 2022, Deputy Aubrey Phillips was the last deputy to die while on duty. On February 12, 2022, while working as a Dublin police officer, she conducted a traffic stop. After arresting the driver, as she was in her vehicle, she suffered an acute medical emergency. Another deputy present began lifesaving efforts, but unfortunately, she passed away later that day at a local hospital.

Two

PLACES

COURTHOUSES, JAILS, AND STATIONS

Having law enforcement jurisdiction throughout the unincorporated areas of the county meant the sheriff's office needed facilities in many locations. Since 1853, these facilities have ranged from small, wood-frame buildings in the distant reaches of the county to modern, multistory high rises in downtown Oakland, and have included spaces within courthouses, jails, and civic buildings as well as stand-alone stations and substations. Deputies and staff have worked in well-made, permanent buildings and poorly built leftover World War II facilities, used far beyond their expected lifetimes. And sometimes, staff worked in drafty, unheated tents and wide-open fields. This chapter shows some of the remarkable, as well as quite unremarkable, places deputies and staff have worked.

The most prominent structures sheriff's office staff worked in are the county courthouses. There have been five courthouses in Alameda County's history. The first was built in the first county seat, Alvarado, in 1853. The second courthouse was in San Leandro in 1855, the third was built in East Oakland in 1873, the fourth opened in June 1875 in Oakland, and the fifth was dedicated in September 1936. Since then, several outlying courthouses were built to serve the county in other locations, including Berkeley, Hayward, Dublin, and Fremont.

During the 1800s, the courthouses usually included the jail used by the sheriff. As the county grew, it became necessary to build separate buildings to house the jail and sheriff's operations. The first substantial jail was built in Oakland in 1875 adjacent to the county courthouse. A jail was later included in the 1936 Oakland courthouse, but the county's increasing population and attendant crime required the opening of other facilities. By 1947, jail overcrowding was such a problem that Sheriff Gleason arranged to take over the World War II US Navy disciplinary barracks near Dublin as the new Santa Rita Rehabilitation Center. By the 1980s, overcrowding and aging buildings again required a new jail. The current Santa Rita Jail opened in Dublin in 1989. Another facility, North County Jail in Oakland, opened in 1984.

Patrol stations, or substations, have always been a part of the sheriff's office operations. In the early days, some deputies worked out of their homes or out of local city buildings such as in Livermore or Hayward. Later, the county built its own facilities, such as the Washington and Eden Township substations.

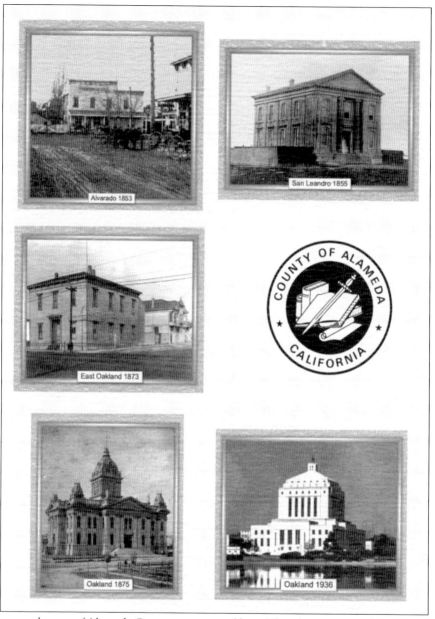

The five courthouses of Alameda County are pictured here. Their location varied with the location of the county seat. There was a fair amount of movement around the county as various groups competed for the political and economic advantage of having the county seat and courthouse in their town. The first courthouse was established with the founding of the county in 1853 in Alvarado, now part of Union City. The second was in San Leandro from 1855 through 1873. Partially destroyed by the 1868 earthquake, it was rebuilt by 1869. In 1873, another county election resulted in the county seat being moved to Oakland, and a new courthouse was built in East Oakland. A larger and more substantial building was finished in 1897 on Broadway between Fourth and Fifth Streets. It served until an even larger and more substantial courthouse was built near Lake Merritt, which opened in 1936 and is still in use. With the county's continued growth, satellite courts were operated in various locations such as Oakland, Hayward, Pleasanton, and Dublin.

The fourth Alameda County Courthouse opened in June 1897 at Fifth Street and Broadway in Oakland. It included the courts and sheriff's offices, a jail, and other county offices, including those of the assessor and tax collector. It and the adjacent county jail occupied the whole block. The building was later demolished. (Author's collection.)

The fifth and current Alameda County Courthouse was dedicated in September 1936. It was larger than the previous building and included courtrooms and the district attorney's office. Originally, it included cells for 100 detainees on the 10th and 11th floors. The building was so representative of the county that, for a time, the image was the centerpiece of the sheriff's office duty patch. It is now known as the Rene C. Davidson Courthouse. (Author's collection.)

BARNET HOTEL

Like the Golden Gate, it is always open. Welcome if you must come, but I advise you not to.

2867 · Alameda County Jail, Oakland, California.

Between 1920 and 1936, besides the many hotels in the city, Oakland had another location to house visitors, the "Barnet Hotel." Its official name was the Alameda County Jail. The jail was of such notoriety that it got its own postcard, probably one in a series highlighting the city's points of interest. From 1920 through 1930, the jail housed people arrested for Prohibition violations.

Behind the Alameda County Courthouse on Broadway in Oakland, the county jail and courthouse were conveniently located for law enforcement activities. The building on the corner of Washington Street and Fourth Street housed the sheriff's office and all related activities, including the county jail. The sheriff operated out of this building until a new courthouse near Lake Merritt opened in 1936.

The office of Sheriff Michael B. Drivers at the county jail building in Oakland was the center of county law enforcement in 1933. Simple furnishings reflect a simpler time, but with changes already evident. An electric floor heater hides in a corner, and Drivers's desk blocks the fireplace previously used to heat the room. A telephone and pen set sit on the desk ready for use.

The Alameda County Jail, pictured in the 1930s, was referred to as the "Barnet Hotel" during the administration of Sheriff Barnet (1920–1936). On Sheriff Gleason's third day in office in 1940, it was the scene of a newsworthy event. An *Oakland Tribune* headline read, "New Sheriff Quells 'Food Riot' of Alien Prisoners, Gleason Tastes, Approves of Disputed Stew, Awes Irate Inmates Back to Order."

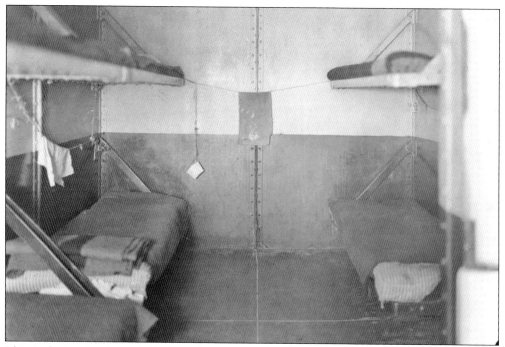

This is the inside of a typical cell at the county jail. It was a substantial and solid building and handled all sheriff's department business in Oakland. At this time, around 1933, there were other jails in outlying cities to hold people arrested by deputies until they could be transported here.

Here is the kitchen on the ground floor of the original Alameda County Jail, showing the tools and cooking methods used from about 1900 through 1930. A pile of meat sits in a pan on the table. Often, prisoners who were trusted would assist in preparing or delivering meals to other prisoners.

On Sunday, September 6, 1936, the new Alameda County Courthouse and Hall of Records at 1225 Fallon Street was dedicated. The *Oakland Tribune* noted, "The district attorney's office occupies the entire ninth floor." The jail and associated support facilities were on the 10th and 11th floors. The building opened for business in October. (University of California, Berkeley, Library.)

Here is the "front door" to the jail facilities in the county courthouse in Oakland. Welcoming all who entered, Sheriff Gleason's name is displayed prominently on the door. An *Oakland Tribune* article published on the dedication day in September 1936 noted that it was "a complete jail, and the necessary adjuncts, for prisoners awaiting trial, is provided on the tenth and eleventh floors. . . . Accommodations are provided for 110 prisoners."

The new 1936 courthouse and jail included an updated and upgraded kitchen and dining facilities. This unique view shows cooks and assistants preparing a meal for the inmates. Deputies and other jail staff also ate food prepared in this kitchen. This photograph was taken sometime around 1958.

The stark interior of the inmates' dining area in the Alameda County Courthouse on Fallon Street is seen here sometime close to opening day. The "Court House Jail," as it was known, opened in 1937 on the 10th floor. Originally designed to hold 120 men, it sometimes housed more.

A deputy prepares paperwork in this 1940s view of the processing area in the jail. Behind him is a cell used for interviews with prisoners. Even though the jail and the building were relatively new, the working space was beginning to get crowded. The county's increasing population and the lingering effects of the Great Depression meant increasing crime.

This is another view of the jail's work area. On the wall at left is the board showing each inmate's location and cell number. In a time before computers and automation, boards such as this provided all the key information deputies needed to know at a glance. With prisoners attending trials and meetings in the building with investigators or attorneys, there was constant movement.

In old crime movies, there is usually a scene where the arrested person is told, "You can make one phone call." At the time those movies were made, in the 1930s through 1950s, this was where one would go to make that call in the jail area of the Alameda County Courthouse near Lake Merritt. The partitions on the wall separate the telephones.

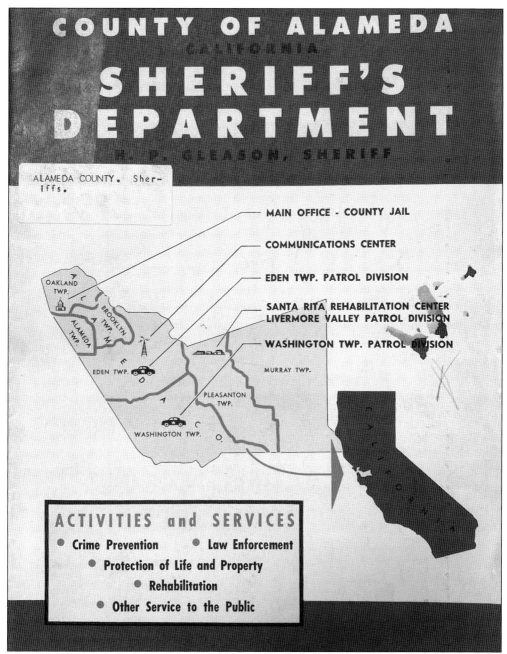

COUNTY OF ALAMEDA
CALIFORNIA
SHERIFF'S
DEPARTMENT
H. P. GLEASON, SHERIFF

ALAMEDA COUNTY. Sheriffs.

MAIN OFFICE - COUNTY JAIL

COMMUNICATIONS CENTER

EDEN TWP. PATROL DIVISION

SANTA RITA REHABILITATION CENTER
LIVERMORE VALLEY PATROL DIVISION

WASHINGTON TWP. PATROL DIVISION

OAKLAND TWP.

BROOKLYN TWP.

ALAMEDA TWP.

ALAMEDA

EDEN TWP.

MURRAY TWP.

PLEASANTON TWP.

WASHINGTON TWP.

CALIFORNIA

ACTIVITIES and SERVICES
- Crime Prevention   • Law Enforcement
- Protection of Life and Property
- Rehabilitation
- Other Service to the Public

In the 1950s, Sheriff Gleason made efforts to explain the role of his office to Alameda County citizens. This included not just describing the activities and services provided, but also the locations of the main offices throughout the county. Inside, this document included a brief description of their lesser-known activities, such as the constables, mounted posse, air squadron, and law enforcement mutual aid.

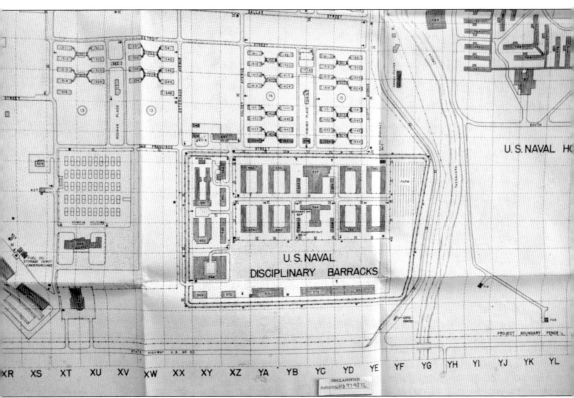

After consultation with local Navy officials, Alameda County formally asked to acquire the US Naval Disciplinary Barracks at Camp Shoemaker near Dublin in August 1946. Sheriff Gleason believed the brig, as it was informally known, would be an economical and adequate start for a new county jail. The property included over 1,000 acres between Camp Parks and Tassajara Road along what was then US Highway 50 (now Interstate 580). It also extended north to the Alameda/Contra Costa border. Besides the brig and associated buildings, small houses formerly used by the base commander and senior officers were rented to deputies who worked at the jail.

This aerial view of Santa Rita Jail is possibly from the 1970s. At this time, the area was still empty except for abandoned buildings left over from when the Navy operated Camp Shoemaker and Shoemaker Naval Hospital. Remnants of the hospital can still be seen on the right. The wide-open spaces were used for raising crops and farm animals, which fed staff and inmates at the jail. Mount Diablo can be seen in the background. US Highway 50 is near the bottom. The large, open area above the highway was known as the grinder. Lower-security barracks with courtyards are at center. The maximum-security Greystone Building is on the left. The original Santa Rita Jail closed in 1989. The new jail occupied a site closer to the hills in the background. By the 2000s, the former jail had been replaced by commercial businesses and housing.

Sheriff Gleason inspects Greystone, the maximum-security building at the former US Naval Disciplinary Barracks in 1947. During World War II, the Navy used the facility to house sailors who committed crimes while stationed at the nearby Camp Parks, Camp Shoemaker, and Shoemaker Naval Hospital. Also during the war, German prisoners of war were housed in some of the buildings in the disciplinary barracks. The Navy closed the camps in late 1946. Sheriff Gleason asked the government to lease the site to Alameda County for a new jail complex. This visit was part of the acquisition of the site to be used for what would initially be called the Santa Rita Rehabilitation Center. Later, it became known as Santa Rita, the Alameda County Jail. Inmates simply called it "Rita."

Here is a view of the main entrance to the original Santa Rita Rehabilitation Center in the late 1950s or early 1960s showing some of the abandoned buildings on the right. Much of the land around the jail included buildings and structures from the former Navy base at Camp Shoemaker and the Shoemaker Naval Hospital. Also to the right is the course of Tassajara Creek.

This is the exterior of Greystone, the maximum-security building. Alameda County took possession of the former US Navy Disciplinary Barracks in 1947. Sheriff Gleason thought the buildings and grounds would be a cost-effective means of expanding the county jail, which was overcrowded. It would also allow him to assess his rehabilitation theories, offering inmates vocational training in an agricultural setting. The jail also offered a public treatment center for alcoholism.

At one of the deputy sheriff's duty stations in Greystone, paperwork was completed at the desk overlooking the cells underneath. The wooden desk, manual typewriter, and rotary dial telephone are indicators of the times. It is likely the desk was Navy surplus and came with the building.

The original Santa Rita Jail included elements left over from its previous service as disciplinary barracks. One of them was that the maximum-security building, Greystone, featured cell ceilings of only heavy-gauge steel mesh. Deputies were stationed above and conducted surveillance during their shifts by looking down into the cells. They would walk the catwalks to ensure every inmate was accounted for.

Here is a look down into a cell at Greystone. The ceiling was open except for the security mesh. Deputies were instructed to look into the cells several times during their shifts.

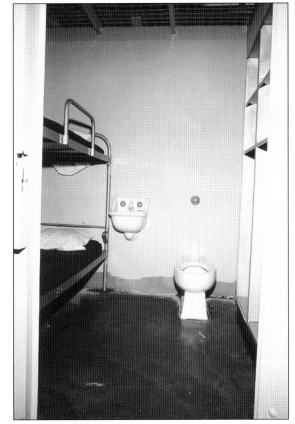

Here is another view into a cell at Greystone. The maximum-security cells had one double bunk bed, one sink, one toilet, and an open cabinet for the two inmates' possessions. Each door was solid, with only one small sliding window, which could only be opened by a deputy. The jail closed in 1989.

This image looks down the main corridor of Greystone. Unlike earlier Alameda County jails, the doors were solid hardwood. The facility reflected the Navy's standards for temporary construction and temporary confinement. It was designed to last only for the duration of World War II.

By the 1950s, Sheriff Gleason had reason to celebrate his management of the sheriff's department. His efforts to build the county jail into an efficient and economical operation were working. It was nearly self-sufficient, saving the county money. The Santa Rita Rehabilitation Center started receiving state-wide praise as a well-managed, model correctional facility. This 1953 *San Francisco Chronicle* front-page article was titled, "The Story of Alameda County Jail–The Best."

This was known as "Main Street" at Santa Rita Jail, also known as First Street. Most of the buildings were World War II–era wooden structures. This view looking east shows the clinic on the left with the prisoner area on the right. At upper left, part of one of the guard towers can be seen. To the right are the prison chapel, mess hall, and auditorium.

Prominently displayed on Main Street is the Santa Rita Jail clock that commemorates Sheriff Gleason's tenure. The clock survived the 1906 earthquake on Market Street in San Francisco. Later, it stood on Broadway in Oakland. In 1963, Hudson Jewelers donated it to Santa Rita Jail. The clock now stands outside the main entrance of the current jail.

For years, the grounds near the Santa Rita Jail housed several other sheriff's office activities. Located in this World War II building was the training division, crime laboratory, and jail administration. The grounds around the jail offered space for firearms training, and the nearby ranges and open space provided room for other training.

Throughout the late 1940s and 1950s, fire departments were few and far between in eastern Alameda County. The Santa Rita Jail Fire Department was an important asset in responding to fires and accidents in the areas outside Livermore and Pleasanton. It responded to many car accidents along the increasingly busy Highway 50, especially after it grew from a two-lane highway to a four-lane expressway. (Sheriff's archive.)

For years after 1947, the Santa Rita Jail firehouse was the closest firefighting unit to Dublin along Highway 50. A posting to the firehouse was a much-desired assignment for inmates. They operated, lived, and ate as a unit under the direction of a deputy. Their equipment included the former Navy firefighting vehicles and buildings.

STAFFED BY INMATES UNDER A DEPUTY SHERIFF
ASSIGNED AS FIRE CHIEF
SANTA RITA FIREHOUSE

The first Alameda County prison farm was in San Leandro near Fairmont Drive. The second farm was part of Santa Rita. In the 1950s, much of the meat and vegetables served to prisoners and staff at the jail came from farms worked by inmates. It was reported that the food harvested by the inmates resulted in some of the best, or at least freshest, meals ever served in a correctional institution.

A major aspect of the original Santa Rita Rehabilitation Center was providing inmates with an opportunity to learn new skills as an alternative to their already-developed criminal capabilities. Many of the skills were agricultural. Here, a local Dublin rancher by the name of Frederiksen oversees an inmate shearing one of the sheep on the jail's grounds.

Inmates harvest crops in the fields east of the Santa Rita Rehabilitation Center. After 1947, the progressive correctional philosophy was that learning vocational skills and having some productive work could lower the probability that inmates would return to criminal activity after their jail terms. In Alameda County, which still included a large farm economy, the skills taught here often related to agriculture and animal husbandry.

It is not often a deputy sheriff is seen running a harvester. This was one of the more unusual jobs at the Santa Rita Rehabilitation Center. Sheriff Gleason's grand plan was to have a nearly self-supporting jail that grew its own food and offered prisoners the opportunity to learn a new trade. How viable those new trades would be in a rapidly urbanizing county was problematical in the 1950s.

In 1958, the Santa Rita Jail was substantially self-sufficient in terms of food. Cattle and hogs were raised on site, vegetables and fruit grew in fields nearby, and food preparation took place at the jail. Prisoners could learn new farming, ranching, and other skills as part of the philosophy of rehabilitation through work. (Sheriff's archive.)

HAZARDOUS DEVICES
RANGE
RESTRICTED AREA
USE OF THIS RANGE IS PROHIBITED UNLESS
ACCOMPANIED BY A SHERIFF'S DEPT EOD RANGEMASTER
F.I.MADIGAN SHERIFF

At the time this photograph was taken, sometime after 1963 and before 1975, the Hazardous Devices Range provided a remote and safe place to handle explosive devices and conduct training. It is still located in the hills beyond the Santa Rita Jail. Residential development gradually expanded nearby over the years, and residents in Dublin can now sometimes hear the results of the bomb squad training behind the hills surrounding the range.

In August 1975, the Santa Rita Jail grounds became a film location when scenes for the made-for-television film *Farewell to Manzanar* were shot there. The wide-open spaces and desolate grounds around the jail simulated the terrain and buildings of a World War II Japanese American internment camp. Mock guard towers and false front buildings were constructed for the filming.

This 1984 aerial view looking west shows the location of the original Santa Rita Jail near the intersection of Interstate 580 and Tassajara Road in Dublin. It was already planned that the World War II–era facility was going to be replaced. By 1989, the new jail was built just to the right of the area marked Santa Rita Rehabilitation Center Replacement Center.

Here are the Office of Emergency Services buildings in San Leandro around 1982. The civil defense and disaster office started in July 1950. At the time, concerns centered on preparing for and dealing with an enemy (likely Soviet Union) attack on the United States. Over time, this threat lessened, and natural and human-made disasters, especially earthquakes and fires, became the predominant concerns. The sheriff's office took the lead in planning for and reacting to these events.

Following World War II, federal, state, and local government officials realized that the United States was not well prepared to defend its population against attack. When the Soviet Union exploded a nuclear weapon in 1949, there was a new emphasis on civil defense. The sheriff's department became the lead agency in the county to organize emergency services. This early version of an emergency operations center shows some of those initial efforts.

The original location of the Alameda County Civil Defense and Disaster office was on 150th Avenue in the hills above San Leandro. The program started in July 1950 with the formation of the sheriff's reserve. Reacting to the implications of the Cold War, civil defense efforts were started throughout the country. Federal government resources, including land and equipment, were made available to local governments. Alameda County assigned civil defense responsibilities to the sheriff's office.

One of the advantages the sheriff's office had after World War II was its access to surplus Navy buildings. Sheriff Gleason took advantage of not only the former disciplinary barracks (which became Santa Rita Jail), but also the buildings nearby. The Northern California Regional Training Center occupied a former noncommissioned officers' club. Many deputies and their families were able to rent and live in former officers' quarters.

The Washington Township substation opened in October 1951 at Centerville, in southern Alameda County. The office was responsible for law enforcement in Washington Township and had 23 deputies and staff. Capt. Richard F. Condon was the first officer in charge of the substation. It closed in 1958.

On October 22, 1951, the Washington Township Substation staff pose for a first day photograph. From left to right are Deputy Russ Wilson, Constable Henry Vervais, Det. Lowell Creighton, Lt. Joe Sheehan, Detective Ev King, Capt. Dick Condon, secretary Dorothy Johnson, Deputies Bill Lawson, Al Silvey, Bud Fall, Fred Turra, Larry White, Dean Davenport, and Bob Klein; Constable Bob Moore; Deputies Jim Chisolm, Bob Swaynie, Tom Bunting, and Hollis Turner; and Sgts. William Hildebrand, Jack Abernathy, and John Dobbins. Deputy Fred Evely was absent.

On the day it closed, June 30, 1958, 24 of the approximately 28 staff pose outside the Washington Township substation. Some would stay on in the sheriff's department while others joined the expanding Fremont Police Department. The substation closed because the City of Fremont assumed jurisdiction once it annexed much of the area in southern Alameda County.

Soon after being organized in 1853, Alameda County was subdivided into townships. The sheriff had primary law enforcement responsibilities outside incorporated cities and set up substations in various locations. One was in Eden Township. The patrol area included the communities of Ashland, Castro Valley, Cherryland, Fairview, San Lorenzo, and Russell City. The Eden Township station had several locations over the years, including one in the Hayward civic buildings. Now it is at 15001 Foothill Boulevard in San Leandro.

Since its start in 1947, the Regional Training Center has provided training to thousands of law enforcement officers throughout the county and state. Its constantly evolving curriculum matches improvements in equipment, policies, procedures, and practices available to law enforcement through the years. This was its location after 1989 on Madigan Road in Dublin.

Castro Valley is one of the fastest-growing unincorporated communities in Alameda County. Despite several attempts to incorporate, the community continues to prefer its unincorporated status. The sheriff's office has responsibility for protecting and serving over 66,000 residents there. Here, Deputy Floyd Gill, the first school resource officer, poses in front of Castro Valley High School with his patrol car, probably in the 1990s.

Many sheriff's department events took place at Frank Youell Field in Oakland. Built at 900 Fallon Street in 1962 as a temporary football field for the Oakland Raiders, the team used it until the Oakland Coliseum was available in 1966. The county courthouse and the Kaiser Convention Center are in the background. Demolished in 1969, the field is now the location of a Laney College parking lot.

The original Santa Rita Jail had guard towers around the perimeter of the facility. When the jail was demolished after 1989, most of the guard towers were destroyed. Volunteers at the sheriff's archive decided to use leftover parts and recreate one. It now stands as an interpretive museum exhibit behind the current Santa Rita Jail.

One of the few remaining artifacts of the original Santa Rita Jail, this cell block door is also one of the very few remaining pieces of the Navy Disciplinary Barracks that later became the Santa Rita Jail. It controlled access into and out of one of the cellblocks from 1947 through 1989, when the jail closed. The sheriff's office staff salvaged it sometime in the early 2000s after the jail was demolished.

The Glenn E. Dyer Building in Oakland, more commonly known as the North County Jail, was built in 1987. The facility closed in 2019 due to budgetary issues and prisoners were moved to Santa Rita Jail. The building is currently empty, and plans for it have not been finalized.

By the 1980s, the original Santa Rita Jail was overcrowded and in poor condition. A new jail was designed to replace it, including sufficient space and reflecting current prison building standards. This is a view of the current jail, about one mile northwest of the original jail site. The new jail opened in 1989. It is one of the larger jails in California and has a capacity of over 3,400 inmates.

A Dublin Police Department patrol car is parked at the entrance to the Santa Rita Jail in Dublin. Alameda County deputies are assigned to Dublin as part of a contract with the city. Law enforcement contracts are also in place with AC Transit, Oakland International Airport, and Highland Hospital.

Among its other duties, the sheriff's office provides animal control services for the county. The animal shelter moved from San Leandro to become the East County Animal Shelter in Dublin in 1996. The newer facility was purpose-built to shelter and care for animals.

Three

EVENTS

DEMONSTRATIONS, DISASTERS, CRIMES, AND COMMUNITY

Beyond the day-to-day stories deputies and staff tell each other, there are events that become defining moments for people or organizations. An organization such as the sheriff's office tends to remember or commemorate many difficult, often tragic, situations. Other times, the stories are humorous. Sometimes, they are just about the unusual things that happen only in a law enforcement environment. Included in this chapter are a few of the events that have special meaning for the office. Also shown here are some of the offbeat events that just happened to be found in the sheriff's archive files.

For the Alameda County Sheriff's Office, several events had major effects on the organization. They include the largest single loss of life by deputy sheriffs in 1898, demonstrations and riots around the county in the 1960s through 1980s, the recovery of kidnapped children and investigation of the Chowchilla Case in 1976, and the Loma Prieta earthquake of 1989. Other critical events, including the two most recent deaths by on-duty deputies, can be found in chapter one.

Among the offbeat events documented here are the cattle roping incident of 1957, the two-week underground fallout shelter test using Santa Rita Jail prisoners in 1959, and the *Mythbusters* television show fiasco of 2011.

Interspersed with these photographs are others that reflect interesting aspects of the lives of law enforcement officers and staff in Alameda County.

SIX BLOWN TO ETERNITY

THE DEATH ROLL.

CHARLES WHITE, eldest son of Sheriff White.
GUS KOCH, Constable of Oakland Township.
J. J. LERRI, Deputy Sheriff.
GEO. C. WOODSUM, Deputy Sheriff, Berkeley.
D. C. CAMERON, Deputy Sheriff.
MRS. HILL, of San Francisco.
The murderous Chinese was also killed.

Murderous Chinese Fires th Fuse Works' Magazine.

Held at Bay, He Causes the Explosio Which Kills Five Officers, One Woman and Blows Himself Into Atoms.

This morning at 5:18 o'clock the works of the Western Fuse and Explosives Company at Melrose, east of Fruitvale, were blown to atoms by a Chinese oper ve, who, after murdering a brother Celestial yesterday, took refuge in the powder magazine of the place. At the hour mentioned he offered to surrender, an when deputy sheriffs went to receive him, he fired the magazine. The explosion blew the murderer and Deputies White, Cameron, Woodsum, Koch and Lerri in ternity. Mrs. Hill of San Francisco was also killed. Forty houses around were wrecked.

Gung Ung Chung, who was employed in the works, had killed Ham Ri Sing yesterday afternoon in a quarrel over Chinese lottery tickets. He then defied the officers of the law who went to arrest him. The murderer fled into the magazine, which contained five tons of giant powder, barricaded the door and threatened to blow up the magazine if any one came to arrest him.

This morning at 5 o'clock Deputy Sheriff Chas. White, with several of the others, returned from breakfast and spoke to him. The Chinese said he wanted to talk with him. White and the others approached him, when the ex plosion took place. This was at 5:18 o'clock. In an instant a terrific ex plosion occurred, killing Deputies White, Koch, Wood

ED. WHITE DESCRIBES THE AWFUL DISASTER.

Deputy Sheriff Ed. White, one of the two men who escaped from the slaughter in a most remarkable manner,

RESCUE OF A WOMAN

Charles Roman also rises Mrs. was one. He was blown toward her by numbering the pressure of before in Explosion before arises the white, who then a bite of debris rushed across the street and, drawing of George Orbits, the Hopi street one keeper. She had remained in the din all night. This is the same house where

The single deadliest day for the Alameda County Sheriff's Department occurred on July 19, 1898, near Oakland. While trying to arrest an alleged murderer, several officers, a visitor staying nearby, a suspect, and some workers were all killed when a Western Fuse and Explosives Company building exploded. The suspect had barricaded himself inside for hours, warning that he would blow everything up if anyone approached. Different newspapers reported different accounts of what caused the tremendous explosion, with several stating the suspect ignited gunpowder inside the building. According to the *Oakland Tribune*, the dead included Sheriff White's son Deputy Charles White, along with Deputies J.J. Lerri, George C. Woodsum, and D.C. Cameron, plus Oakland Township constable Gus Koch and Sadie Hill. Hill had refused to evacuate, even after nearby residents were warned about the situation. Another paper indicated four Chinese workers at the facility died in the explosion. The name of the suspect was variously reported as Gung Chong, Chung, or Goon Ng Chung. He was a suspect in a murder the day before and had sought refuge at the company where he worked.

Nov 1913.

In November 1913, Constable Manuel Borge (second from left) had the opportunity to have his photograph taken with Sheriff Barnet (far right) and two other men outside the Alameda County Jail in Oakland. The occasion was the transfer of a prisoner, Robert Bradley (handcuffed, second from right), an escapee from the jail, the convicted murderer of Oakland special police officer Charles A. Williams, and guilty of robbery. Constable Borge later escorted the prisoner to Folsom State Prison.

This is a c. 1933 crime scene. Photographic evidence became an important part of investigations soon after portable cameras became available. Here, the broken window of a car abandoned on an Alameda County street shows where a bullet passed through. The image comes from a glass plate negative, one of the early practical forms of photography.

Here is the scene of another crime, as captured on a glass plate negative in 1920. The image shows the means of entry and the burglary tools used to break open the safe. Alameda County was an early adopter of advanced crime-solving techniques and technology.

In early 1942, in accordance with Executive Order 9066, federal, state, and local law enforcement agencies began seizing contraband property. Here, Sheriff Gleason poses with other officers in Hayward with the results of those seizures. Firearms, radios, and cameras, mostly from Japanese American citizens in Alameda County, are displayed. Later that year, the federal government detained and moved Japanese Americans and their families to internment camps. (Alameda County Deputy Sheriff's Association.)

Even as late as 1957, department staff could be called upon to perform actions reminiscent of Wild West deputies. This young steer was running down a street in Hayward one night and was chased by a California Highway Patrol car. Sheriff's department night detective Tom Houchins responded to the call and successfully roped the beast and brought it to a halt. Detective Houchins later became Sheriff Houchins.

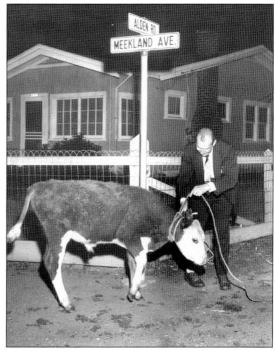

For two weeks in December 1959, five deputies and eighty-nine Santa Rita Jail inmates participated in an underground fallout shelter exercise. This Naval Radiological Defense Laboratory test took place at Camp Parks to evaluate what would happen to a group confined underground in the aftermath of a nuclear attack. Walmer "Jerry" Strope, the experiment leader, leads the group to the shelter in this photograph.

Obviously happy to be nearly done with their two-week experiment, the 89 inmates laugh for a posed photograph. Each participant wore a numbered bib so staff could record their reactions to extended underground living. The experiment was meant to observe people's responses to living in fallout shelters. (Sheriff's archive.)

Inmates exit the fallout shelter after a two-week experiment in December 1959. The inmates were all volunteers and were accompanied by several deputy sheriffs and staff of the US Radiological Defense Laboratory. Several stayed for the whole time, even though their sentences ended during the test.

A reserve deputy sheriff looks on with amusement as he is awarded the "Fallout Shelter" trophy. The incorporation of an outhouse as part of the trophy is appropriate, based on participants' reports of the smell that developed inside the shelter during the two-week experiment. Sheriff Gleason appears less amused. The award ceremony took place in 1960.

This is a group photograph of Sheriff Gleason with reserve deputy sheriffs. The Fallout Shelter outhouse trophy suggests this was a humorous award ceremony for those who took part in the experiment in 1959. There is no indication of why they all look so glum, except perhaps that they did not have fond memories of being confined underground with over 80 inmates for two weeks.

One of a series of promotional or training images, this photograph shows a time-honored ritual at the beginning of a shift when a deputy signs out a vehicle from the duty sergeant. The building in the background shows that the image was taken at the substation at the Santa Rita Jail. The fact that the vehicle is white indicates it was one of the training cars.

Often overshadowed by later demonstrations and riots in Berkeley in 1968, riot duty started in earnest the year before. In October 1967, demonstrators massed at the US Army Induction Center at 1515 Clay Street in Oakland to prevent men from being processed into military service. The sheriff's department and other law enforcement personnel acted as escorts for buses through downtown Oakland. (*Oakland Tribune* Collection, Oakland Museum of California.)

This 1960s photograph shows a deputy spraying a stream of tear gas on demonstrators. The incident took place at the University of California, Berkeley campus in Sproul Plaza. This image was featured in newspaper articles reporting on the event. According to some reports, the photograph was altered to emphasize the stream of tear gas. The newspaper later claimed it was done for clarity.

Deputies in riot gear march through Sproul Plaza in April 1970. The sheriff's department, along with other Bay Area law enforcement agencies, provided mutual aid support to the university and Berkeley police departments during demonstrations in the 1960s and 1970s. The causes might change, but demonstrations continue to the present. (*Oakland Tribune* Collection, Oakland Museum of California.)

Demonstrators, or people just attending the event, overturn a car on Bancroft Way in Berkeley in February 1971. The US government license plate drew the attention of part of the crowd, who decided to register their discontent. (*Oakland Tribune* Collection, Oakland Museum of California.)

This photograph shows a deputy ducking a rock thrown by a demonstrator in Berkeley in April 1970. Onlookers also ran from the scene since they were just as likely to be hit with a bottle, brick, or stone. Demonstrations could turn from a peaceful assembly to a violent confrontation or riot in a moment. Then it could just as quickly be peaceful again. (*Oakland Tribune* Collection, Oakland Museum of California.)

Deputies in riot gear rest in People's Park in Berkeley during or after one of the demonstrations nearby. The Alameda County Sheriff's Department was often called in to assist the University of California Police and Berkeley Police Department during these disturbances. Many other Bay Area law enforcement agencies were drawn into the sometimes-violent disagreements between the university, students, and others.

A deputy comforts one of the recently escaped children from what was called the Chowchilla kidnapping in July 1976. After being found by the side of a road near Livermore by an off-duty deputy sheriff and his wife, the 26 children and their bus driver were taken to the Santa Rita Jail. There they were given clean clothes, food, and drink while investigators took statements and contacted parents. The press descended on the jail to get the latest information on what had become a story of international interest.

Collecting evidence of the Chowchilla kidnapping case took months and required a whole new level of crime scene processing for the office. Multiple crime scenes located in different counties resulted in over 4,800 pieces of evidence being collected, packaged, maintained, and inventoried. Even the moving van the driver and children were held in had to be secured.

The moving van and every piece of evidence found in it were taken to a warehouse near Santa Rita Jail. There the investigators poured over every piece trying to determine the suspects' identities, as well as documenting the evidence for use in the trial. The press also wanted to take every photograph they could for the sensational ongoing fugitive hunt.

After their capture, the three suspects were questioned at the Livermore rock quarry, where they had buried the trailer with their captives inside. Pictured here handcuffed next to the jail van they arrived in are, from left to right, Frederick Woods, James Schoenfeld, and Richard Schoenfeld, with their lawyer. They were convicted of kidnapping in 1977 and sentenced to life in prison, but all were eventually paroled. The last one, Woods, was released in 2022.

Probably on July 17, 1976, the day after the bus driver and children escaped, investigators take photos of the entrance hole leading to the buried moving van. The plywood cover, once covering the hole with two tractor batteries and several feet of dirt covering, lies nearby where bus driver Frank Edward "Ed" Ray pushed it aside. The 26 children, aged five to fourteen, and the bus driver were underground for 16 hours before their escape.

A tired and dirty but free Ed Ray is pictured here soon after his transportation to the Santa Rita Jail complex on the night of the escape. Ray was the Dairyland Union School District bus driver who endured a kidnapping but found the courage and resourcefulness to free himself and 26 children from an underground prison.

Originally constructed in World War II by the Navy for training and recreation, the Camp Parks gym was later converted for civilian use. By 1982, it usually hosted local youth athletic events, especially basketball, for Pleasanton, Livermore, and Dublin children. In the 1980s, it was often used to temporarily house overflow numbers of arrested demonstrators.

Deputies wait to arrest demonstrators at Lawrence Livermore National Laboratory during the 1980s. Some of the demonstrations drew thousands. Transporting and housing them at Santa Rita proved difficult and required creative solutions. At one point, tents were set up on county property near the jail to house those arrested.

To manage the considerable number of arrestees at Lawrence Livermore National Laboratory and Sandia National Laboratory demonstrations, many had to be housed in fields near Santa Rita Jail. Tents were rented, some of which were red and white striped. Both arrestees and deputies could be heard referring to the "circus-like" environment.

The unexpectedly considerable number of people who chose to be arrested at demonstrations at Lawrence Livermore National Laboratory resulted in some informal housing and feeding situations. Watched over by deputies, these arrestees stand in line outside for their meal. There were stories that some arrestees viewed their arrest and temporary incarceration as a kind of adventure.

The June 1981 demonstrations at Lawrence Livermore National Laboratory included thousands of attendees. Over 1,200 of them chose to be arrested. The logistics of arresting, transporting, housing, feeding, and legally processing them were enormous. The large gym on the grounds of Camp Parks and other Santa Rita Jail buildings were used for the effort. Men and women were usually housed in different buildings.

This is an example of brochures written to organize protests in the 1980s. A series of peaceful demonstrations against nuclear weapons and their development occurred at Lawrence Livermore. Early events included thousands of demonstrators, many eager to be arrested. This sometimes severely taxed the sheriff's office in terms of housing and adjudication of cases.

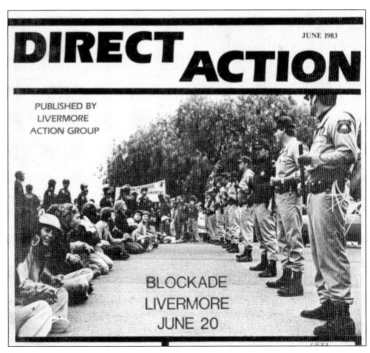

93

By 1981, the original Santa Rita Jail was showing its age and inadequacy. Escapes were not uncommon. As residential building increased just across the highway, the number and severity of escapee crime increased dramatically. Pleasanton residents and officials were irate over the inability, or in their opinion, the unwillingness of the county to take care of the problem. On September 21, this unofficial warning sign appeared on Interstate 580 near the jail. A local newspaper photographer was tipped off to take a picture in time for the next edition. Stories suggest that the sheriff was not amused, and a deputy was directed to make sure the sign came down. To this day, the identity of the sign's creator and installer is a closely kept secret.

Deputies assist in rescue and recovery work on the collapsed portion of Interstate 880 (the Cypress Structure) after the 1989 Loma Prieta earthquake. At 5:04 p.m. on October 17, 1989, a massive magnitude 6.9 earthquake rocked the region. One consequence was the collapse of a two-level, four-lane highway in Oakland. Emergency and law enforcement agencies from the entire area responded to the disaster.

Pictured is the collapsed Cypress Structure portion of I-880 six months after the Loma Prieta earthquake. The collapsed upper level and the twisted steel rebar attest to the power of the quake. From the beginning of the disaster, the sheriff, also the county coroner, and staff worked first on rescue, and later, recovery.

Deputies kept and framed this sign found at a demonstration at People's Park in Berkeley in August 1991. It includes the signatures of the deputies working that day. If taken from a University of California demonstration, it is ironic that "psychopathic" was misspelled. Decades after the event, the sign is one of the artifacts at the sheriff's archive.

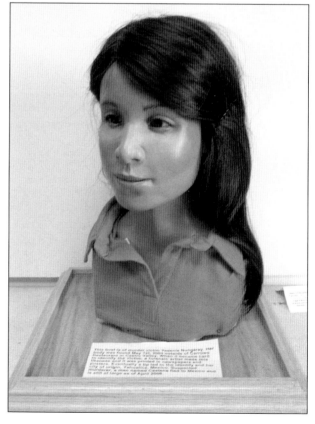

One of the saddest duties deputies face is dealing with unidentified murder victims. In 2003, a body was found in Castro Valley. It seemed as if it would be impossible to determine who the victim was given the condition of the remains. However, using innovative techniques, including a forensic artist and sculptor, this likeness was created. Dedicated and determined investigative efforts by the sheriff's office eventually resulted in the identification of the young woman in 2006. The victim was Yesenia Nungaray Becerra.

TAKING AIM AT MYTHS FOR 10 YEARS!

JUNE 2012 Eric Haven

In December 2011, while filming an episode of the Discovery Channel television show *Mythbusters*, a homemade cannon being tested at the sheriff's office bomb range fired a cannonball, which bounced over an embankment and flew into a Dublin neighborhood. It went 700 feet, crashed through a house, and ended up in a nearby parked minivan. No one was injured. *Mythbusters* often used the bomb range for filming.

Another hazard for deputies is car accidents. The causes vary, but include high-speed chases, drunken or impaired civilian drivers, poorly maintained rural roads, dense fog, wet or icy streets, or just bad luck. Patrolling the distant reaches of over 821 square miles also means that any assistance might take a long time, especially at night. In this case, Deputy P.J. Kennedy's patrol car was hit by a drunk driver in 1989.

Some of the other duties performed by deputies are often forgotten. The sheriff's department often promoted bicycle safety through programs with local school districts. Part of the program included marking bicycles to help identify the owner in case of a theft. Here, a deputy works with two students at an event.

Four

EQUIPMENT

UNIFORMS, TRANSPORTATION, RADIOS, AND GEAR

To the public, one of the first impressions upon meeting an Alameda County deputy sheriff is the uniform and gear they wear. The distinctive uniform, badge, gun and holster, and gear on the belt all signify immediately that the person is a law enforcement officer. This chapter shows vehicles, insignia, uniforms, and other gear used by the deputies and staff over the years.

To the deputies, the uniform, the vehicle, the equipment in it, and all the other gear are not just tools of the trade, but often the potential difference between life and death. And all that equipment comes with a set of comforts and discomforts that must be borne all shift long. At the same time, the badge, uniform, and equipment convey authority, responsibility, and pride.

For all those reasons and more, equipment is an incredibly important aspect of deputies' experiences. For the Alameda County Sheriff's Office, equipment has changed dramatically from six-guns and horses to the latest high technology. Over the decades, much has changed. Purpose-made uniforms replaced personally owned clothes. Cars, motorcycles, airplanes, and helicopters replaced horses. Semiautomatic pistols and rifles replaced revolvers and shotguns. Digital communications and radios replaced the telephone and the call box. On the following pages are different pieces of gear used by the sheriff's office.

On April 23, 1907, the Alameda County Board of Supervisors approved the purchase of an automobile for the sheriff. The Pioneer Automobile Company sold the county a 40-horsepower Model C-11 Thomas automobile for $3,280.10, a substantial amount at the time. Shown outside the Alameda County Courthouse in Oakland are, from left to right, (front seat) Sheriff Barnet and Deputy Jack Collier; (back seat) Chief Deputy John H. Reilly, Deputy Ed Sweeney, and chief jailer Pete White.

Sheriff's department staff admire the new vehicle parked near the county jail in Oakland. While there is no date on this photograph, it was likely taken in the early 1900s. Even then, it was prestigious for the department to have the latest technology, especially considering the long distances involved in traveling throughout the county.

By November 1913, the sheriff's department had purchased at least one upgraded car. Here, Constable Manuel Borge (left) from Eden Township poses with a deputy outside the Alameda County Jail in Oakland. Automobiles proved to be a marked improvement over horses and buggies.

In the 1930s, the only organized fire protection service outside Livermore and Pleasanton was the Alameda County Fire Patrol. Part of the sheriff's office, its employees were not salaried but paid by the fire. At one time, it became known that one employee was increasing his pay by igniting small brush fires. He was fired. Here is a new truck in July 1938. (Livermore Heritage Guild.)

Following World War II, the sheriff's department took advantage of the volunteers and deputies who had pilot's licenses and aircraft. The county had many small airports and airfields that allowed the department to take advantage of the speed and ease of air transport. The squadron flew staff for local official duties. Sometimes, pilots transported prisoners and landed on one of the old Camp Shoemaker roads at Santa Rita Jail. On one map in the sheriff's archive, the road is marked as the

"4th Street Air Strip." A 1958 sheriff's office booklet noted, "Spear-heading the trend of modern law enforcement, the sheriff has, for the past nine years commanded the Sheriff's Air Squadron . . . [the pilots] have responded at all hours to assist in searching for missing persons, escaped prisoners, or planes downed in the rugged terrain of southern Alameda County."

Floyd Heffton (left) and another deputy stand next to their then state-of-the-art patrol vehicle. Mounted on the back bumper is a radio antenna. The sheriff's department cars started to be equipped with radios in the late 1930s. Originally only one-way, deputies would stop and use the nearest available coin-operated telephone booth for additional information. Radio communication often proved to be immensely helpful while patrolling remote parts of the county.

Founded about 1940, the sheriff's mounted posse had various names, including the sheriff's mounted patrol. Its primary job was ceremonial, and it was a regular feature of Alameda County parades, rodeos, and other events. The award-winning posse has also appeared in national parades such as the Rose Bowl in Pasadena, California. For a period in the late 1950s, the posse had an auxiliary band.

In 1955, staff pose outside the Washington Township station. The station managed patrol and cases in and around what is now Fremont, California. From left to right are Detectives Henry Vervais and Henry "Hank" Marks, Deputies Orren Strand, Russ Wilson, and Larry White, Lt. Joe Sheehan, Capt. Don Condon, and Deputies Richard Hess, Dick Souza, and Jim Wilson. Not pictured is Deputy Bob Swayne.

Volunteers practice during an emergency response exercise in the 1960s. Civil defense preparedness became an even more important responsibility for the sheriff's office following World War II. Planning for possible Cold War attacks became an added responsibility to earthquake and fire preparation—always an issue in California.

In the background, volunteers practice entering and recovering victims from a second-floor room. The equipment and vehicles were state of the art for the post–World War II period. Almost all items were surplus from World War II and donated to Alameda County by the federal government.

Here is a collection of sheriff's office vehicles. The motorcycles are used for traffic enforcement and ceremonial situations. The all-terrain vehicle is useful for search and rescue duties in the very rugged rural areas of the county. The car is still the typical vehicle used for patrol.

Like most American law enforcement agencies, the sheriff's office bought and operated Harley-Davidson motorcycles. Here, three deputies pose outside the main entrance of the Eden Township station on Foothill Boulevard in San Leandro, probably in the 1980s. Deputy Tom Rodrigues is at far right.

Offroad motorcycles were the 20th-century equivalent of 19th-century horses. The far reaches of Alameda County are still as rugged as they have always been. And they still need to be patrolled. Shown from left to right are Deputies Chuck Farrugia, Dale Benny, and Pat Adams in about 1983. They were among the first members of the Offroad Motorcycle Patrol Unit.

This clock and car both come from earlier times in sheriff's office history. The clock came to its current location after being on Market Street in San Francisco, Broadway in Oakland, and on the main street of the original Santa Rita Jail. The restored 1949 Nash squad car is owned by the Deputy Sheriff's Association. Both are pictured here outside the current Santa Rita Jail in Dublin.

In 1982, Dublin became an incorporated city. It needed a police department to protect and serve the small community of approximately 15,000 residents. To keep city government costs low, the city decided to contract with the Alameda County Sheriff's Office for police services. Later that year, sheriff's office patrol cars, with hastily attached Dublin Police signs, were seen on the city streets.

One of the sheriff's office explosive ordnance disposal unit vehicles is pictured here with its trailer. The trailer holds a shield and explosive containment device. This image features equipment used in 1996. The background shows that there were still many old World War II–era Navy and original Santa Rita Jail buildings in eastern Dublin.

Alameda County Sheriff Coroner's Bureau staff member Tim Buckhoot stands in front of the coroner's van in the 1970s. The coroner's bureau is responsible for determining the time and cause of death in cases of sudden or unexpected deaths. In Alameda County, the sheriff and coroner functions are combined in one elected position. The Oakland Public Library is in the background.

Starting in 1947, prisoners housed at Santa Rita Jail often had a long drive before they could appear at the Alameda County Courthouse in Oakland. Here is the transportation staff and their vehicles on display at Santa Rita in 1959. In the background are two of the guard towers that stood around the outside of the jail's grounds.

Here are examples of some of the more recent vehicles used to transport prisoners. Most days, deputies collect prisoners from Santa Rita Jail, load them onto vehicles like these, and take them to various locations throughout the county for court appearances or to meet with attorneys.

The sheriff's office's responsibility for waterways extends halfway across San Francisco Bay. The Maritime Unit received this vessel after September 11, 2001, to help patrol those waters. It was eventually determined to be too costly to maintain and operate, so the unit now operates smaller vessels while working closely with the US Coast Guard and other law enforcement agencies.

This looks like it could be the setting of an early-20th-century cops and robbers movie. Rolltop wooden desks, Underwood manual typewriters, paper calendars and maps, and candlestick telephones were the tools of the trade for detectives in January 1933. This was one of the offices at the Alameda County Jail in Oakland.

Detectives of the sheriff's department are hard at work on the second floor of the county jail on Washington Street in Oakland. In the late 1930s, this may have been the entire complement of detectives for the county. Soon after this, office space for detectives might also have been found in the then-new Alameda County Courthouse on Fallon Street.

At a time when paperwork actually involved paper, Capt. R.E. Condon works at his desk at the Washington Township Substation in Centerville, California, in October 1956. He is surrounded by all the period-appropriate office technology of the day: a dial telephone, a paper desk calendar, a wall calendar, a two-hole paper punch, and an ink pen. The Steelcase office desk and chairs were standard-issue furniture, but are now considered mid-century modern classics.

Pictured is another example of 1950s law enforcement technology: the manual typewriter, with its standalone table. A deputy is typing out his report at the Washington Township Substation in 1956. The wall map behind him shows the patrol area for the substation, the unincorporated region around Fremont.

In 1942, the dispatcher's desk at the main control station was highlighted in a sheriff's office brochure distributed to the public. Located near San Leandro, the 500-watt main control station operated as station KPDA. It connected to 35 radio-equipped patrol cars, each with 25-watt transmitters. The sheriff noted, "This equipment gives direct two-way radio telephone service to locations in some remote part of the country, where a telephone may be miles away."

At one time, manual typewriters, dial phones, vacuum tube radios, index cards, two-hole punches, staplers, and lots of paper were the tools used in the sheriff's office communications center. This view shows staff hard at work in the Fairmont Drive location in San Leandro. It also shows the hand-me-down former World War II buildings that housed them for many years. Two shotguns are in a rack below the window.

Deputy Arthur "Art" Allen is pictured at his radio dispatch station in 1947. Surrounded by what was high technology at the time, Allen would go on to a lengthy career designing, building, and repairing Alameda County radio communications equipment and systems. He got his job because he came out of the US Navy in World War II with radio experience and a highly sought-after Federal Communications Commission license.

From the early days of radio, the sheriff's department relied on in-house expertise to design, build, maintain, and repair its equipment. The department was one of the early adopters of radios among law enforcement. Given Alameda County's hilly terrain, several hilltop radio repeaters were needed. From left to right are Deputy Charles B. McMurphy, Sheriff Jack Gleason, and Deputy Arthur Allen at the Sunol Ridge repeater tower.

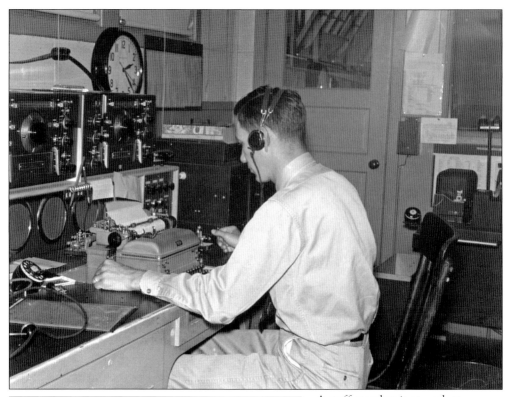

A staff member is at work at KPDA sometime before 1947. The facility was in a three-room wood building behind Fairmont Hospital in San Leandro and broadcast on 1658 kilohertz, with patrol units broadcasting on 35.220 megahertz. Stories circulated in the department that during World War II, dispatchers could occasionally hear the broadcasts of German tanks from North Africa at night.

Deputies Preston A. Dietz (left) and Jack Reidy pose in uniform in 1947. Khaki pants and shirt, dark tie, and dark hat were the work wear up until the 1950s. They stand in front of a privately purchased car used for patrol in the southern reaches of the county. The county provided them with a light and siren, which was added to the car.

Here is a closer look at uniforms, insignia, and badges for the Alameda County Sheriff's Department in 1951. From left to right, Deputies John Dobbins, Bill Hildebrand, and Jack Abernathy pose outside the Washington Township Substation in Centerville. The photograph may have been taken soon after the substation opened.

By 1957, the sheriff's reserve program included 650 men and women who supplemented full-time deputies on patrol. They received 90 hours of basic training and additional training in subsequent years. According to a report that year, they contributed over 60,000 hours of volunteer, unpaid service. The report stated that in addition to patrol duties, "they have served during floods, fires and other natural disasters."

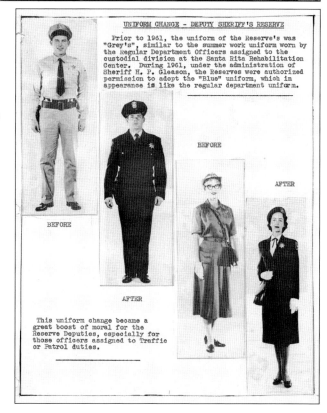

UNIFORM CHANGE - DEPUTY SHERIFF'S RESERVE

Prior to 1961, the uniform of the Reserve's was "Grey's", similar to the summer work uniform worn by the Regular Department Officers assigned to the custodial division at the Santa Rita Rehabilitation Center. During 1961, under the administration of Sheriff H. P. Gleason, the Reserves were authorized permission to adopt the "Blue" uniform, which in appearance is like the regular department uniform.

BEFORE

BEFORE

AFTER

AFTER

This uniform change became a great boost of moral for the Reserve Deputies, especially for those officers assigned to Traffic or Patrol duties.

This might be the first design worn by sheriff's department deputies. It has a shield shape with a dark background, a light-colored bear, a slightly darker landscape, and a green pine tree. It was probably authorized in the early 1950s.

At the same time as the patch above, this slightly different patch was used by sheriff's department staff who worked at Santa Rita Jail. It featured a khaki-colored background worn on khaki uniforms and includes the light-colored bear, darker landscape background, and green pine tree.

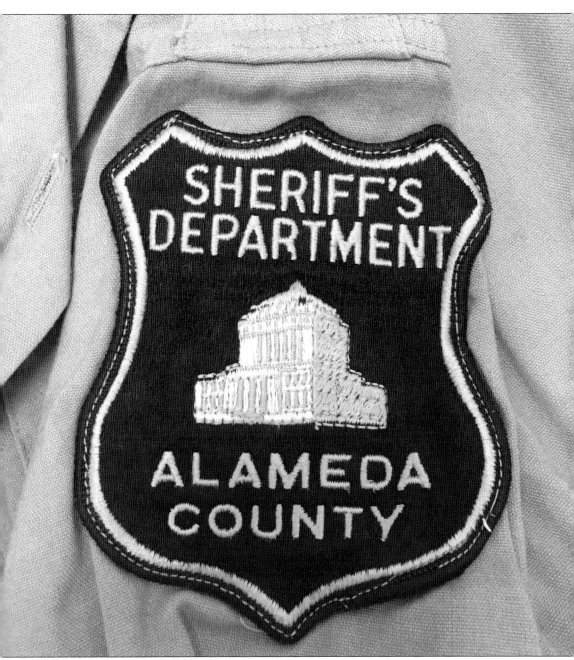

This patch was worn by deputies during the 1970s and replaced the earlier patches with a bear and a tree. The central image is the Alameda County courthouse in Oakland, which opened in 1936. The patch retains the shield shape. There were no variations between the patch worn by deputies and the patch worn by other staff. Like the earlier patches, it was worn on the left shoulder of shirts or jackets.

At some point in the late 1960s, Alameda County deputies working at riots and demonstrations in Berkeley and Oakland acquired the nickname "Blue Meanies." It happened sometime after the Beatles movie *Yellow Submarine* was released in 1968 and referred to bad guys in the movie. The nickname was given to deputies in part because of the odd light blue jumpsuits they wore. Legend has it that the department realized that regular duty uniforms could be damaged during demonstrations. A rushed search for something more appropriate began, and a local hardware store said it could get 200 Ben Davis jumpsuits quickly, but the only color available was light blue. As time went on, the Blue Meanie nickname was applied to all law enforcement officers throughout the United States. Next to the Blue Meanie in this photograph is an example of what female deputies wore at the Santa Rita Jail in the 1950s and 1960s. It was in a shade that might be described as "institutional green."

This is the current duty patch worn by deputies in the sheriff's office. It is a departure from earlier patches that used a shield design. This design added a badge image and the text "Deputy Sheriff" but retained the bear. Other personnel wear different patches identifying them as staff of the sheriff's office.

In 1982, the newly incorporated City of Dublin decided to contract out its police services. After a brief review of several competing bids, the city chose the sheriff's office. Dublin Police Department officers are also Alameda County sheriff's deputies. The Dublin police chief is a commander in the sheriff's office. (Author's collection.)

This is an example of the current sheriff's office badge. Prior to 1928, Alameda County deputy sheriff badges featured a six-pointed star. Sheriff Burton Becker changed the style to a seven-pointed star topped with rounded points. This badge was worn by Deputy William "Bill" Rhodes, who was instrumental in setting up and operating the sheriff's archive. Most of the photographs in this book come from the archive.

A deputy with the bomb squad shows off a full kit during an exercise in 1996. A caption on the back identifies the protective gear as a "Med-Eng" suit. The deputy carries a portable X-ray device to examine suspected devices. Gear and technology constantly evolve in the competition between bomb makers and bomb destroyers.

Explosive ordnance disposal personnel are highly trained for the incredibly dangerous tasks they perform. Over time, training and equipment have improved, increasing the chance of a safe outcome. This deputy is lining up then-state-of-the-art X-ray equipment during a 1996 exercise. During a real event, no photographer would ever be allowed this close to a suspected device.

Seen here is everything one needs to defuse a bomb, all packed up in attaché cases. This was the first-generation toolkit available to the bomb squad in 1973. In the background is a shield used by the bomb squad as well as one of the helmets squad members used at the time.

Sometimes, it is shocking to see how much equipment and practices have changed over the years. As technology improves, so does equipment. Here is some of the original equipment used by the office when it established the explosive ordnance team. A caption on the reverse reads, "ACSO Bomb Squad first generation body armor & 1973 shields."

Using the latest technology has always been a hallmark of the Alameda County Sheriff's Office bomb squad. Here, an explosive ordnance disposal deputy shows off a remotely controlled robot during an exercise. While the state-of-the-art equipment of the 1970s might look archaic now, it was what was available at the time. (Livermore Heritage Guild.)

Alameda County has had a number of businesses that store or use explosives, such as quarries. After World War II, there was always a chance that unexploded bombs or explosives might be found in the county. The sheriff's office often used educational tools like this one to warn children and parents about the hazards of handling or playing with such items.

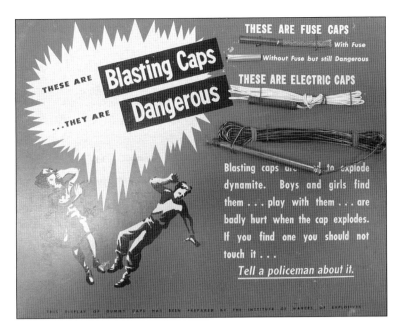

Deputies Rich Lee (foreground) and Barbara Hartman monitor prisoners in the current Santa Rita Jail. The current jail is much safer, more secure, and more comprehensive than the jail that preceded it. In the days of the original jail, sitting at a desk on a catwalk overlooking the maximum-security cells was business as usual. Most deputies today could not imagine the working conditions of the old days.

Recordkeeping is a critical part of law enforcement. In the late 1800s and early 1900s, the technology of photography emerged as a useful way of recording who was arrested and why. It aided law enforcement, since criminals could easily change their names, but changing their appearance was more difficult. Here is a page from one of the many mugshot books used by the sheriff's department for the period between 1914 and 1920. As an emerging practice, deputies often used whatever books or journals they could find and adapted them to this use. In this case, a Register of County Licenses journal became a place to paste photographs of criminals. Unique identifying numbers, crimes, names, and aliases are handwritten for each entry. The crimes listed for the 12 people on pages 240 and 241 range from petit (petty) larceny, through grand larceny, burglary, an unidentified felony, and attempted rape.

Finally, here is some equipment not normally associated with the sheriff's office: football gear. For a brief period in the 1970s and 1980s, law enforcement agencies had unofficial tackle football teams that competed in what were known as "Pig Bowls" at various local football fields. Pig Bowl I was played in 1975 with the sheriff's office deputies (the Lawmen) playing the Hayward Police Department (Hayward Heat). Hayward won 18-7. Here, Deputies Joe Stewart (tackle, No. 75) and Mike Taber (guard, No. 69) are pictured playing during Pig Bowl VII at the California State University Hayward Stadium on January 16, 1982. Pig Bowl VIII also took place in 1982 and was televised on Channel 3. At that game, the sheriff's deputies played the Sacramento Police Department. In 1984, Deputy Michael Petrich collapsed during a game against the Oakland Police Department and later died. It may have been the last game in the series.

DISCOVER THOUSANDS OF LOCAL HISTORY BOOKS FEATURING MILLIONS OF VINTAGE IMAGES

Arcadia Publishing, the leading local history publisher in the United States, is committed to making history accessible and meaningful through publishing books that celebrate and preserve the heritage of America's people and places.

Find more books like this at
www.arcadiapublishing.com

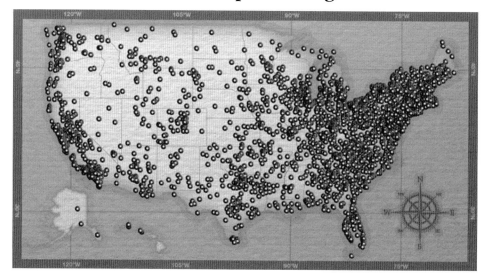

Search for your hometown history, your old stomping grounds, and even your favorite sports team.

Consistent with our mission to preserve history on a local level, this book was printed in South Carolina on American-made paper and manufactured entirely in the United States. Products carrying the accredited Forest Stewardship Council (FSC) label are printed on 100 percent FSC-certified paper.

MADE IN THE